58 Little Things That Have a Big Impact

Published by

Ivy Planning Group, LLC

15204 Omega Drive, Suite 110

Rockville, Maryland 20850

301.963.1669

www.ivygroupllc.com

ISBN 0-97-4152-1-4

D1279797

Printed in the United States of Ame

Book design by Dane Rosendahl

To my guys

Gary II, Alex and Bradley
who keep life fun, challenging, and fulfilling
and Gary
the love of my life

Acknowledgements

I am deeply grateful to the thousands of people who have participated in workshops, classes and learning sessions that have led to this book, and particularly to Denise, Karen, Vhonda, Ed, Antoinette, Betty, Cici, David, Audrey, Tujuanna, Eric, Maria, Teresa, Sheilah, Andy, Sal, Angela, Usha, Jamie, Yvonne, Monica, Lenore, Camille, Ralph, Edie, Sandy, Brenda, Barbara, Gerri, Yartish, Lisa, Ernie, Angel, Michael, John, Robert, Rebecca, Rod, Rob, Karen, Anne, Joerg and Ken. Kudos and appreciation to Mary, Steve, Patrice, Natividad, Sunita and Ed for the opportunities and insights.

Thank you Ivy team for tolerating my Type-A behavior as I doggedly pushed this project, even when your plates were beyond full. Special thanks to Cynthia, Bev, Leslie, Donna, Chris, Hanan, Alan, Camela, Jim, Tayna, Lakisha, Anne, John, Susan, Clara, Ronald, Lauren, Lorraine, Sherisa, Kevin, and Ray for brainstorming, Wild Card tracking, Quiz number crunching and all that was required to make sense of the data.

Thank you Visage (not TEC ☺) #359 for your guidance. Special thanks to Judith Glaser for your leadership and commitment. Kudos to Profiles in Diversity Journal, Diversity Best Practices, IDTV, Diversity Inc., and ASTD for your assistance.

Dane, you are a creative genious - thank you!

Alex, it takes a very special seventeen year old to stand up to his overly assertive mom. Your business acumen is scary fabulous. Thank you for making me listen to you. You made the book better.

Gary, thank you for supporting me, even when it distracts me from you. Your counsel is, as always, wise; your patience unwavering.

The Journey—
How We Got Here....

When we first started to do organizational improvement work we were very focused on systemic change. This meant taking significant new actions. Along the way we learned that subtle actions also matter. Clients have taught us that the details of "how-to" need to be better explained. Well intentioned people need to hear more than "be more inclusive."

A customer introduced Ivy to the concept of micro-messages and microinequities in the '90s. Micro-messages are small, subtle communications that are transmitted by words, signals, tone, and body language. Microinequities are a pattern of negative micro-messages that accumulate to discourage and impair performance. Consulting firms often benefit from their exposure to many clients who are simultaneously seeking to solve similar problems in very different environments. Consultants have the pleasure of working in real-life lab environments. This company had demonstrated its ability to hire a diverse workforce. They sought a new approach to become even more inclusive. Microinequities was a concept that had been discussed in academic settings, but not much if at all in corporate America.

Ivy participated in the design of the microinequities curricula and was tasked to deliver a comprehensive rollout of the workshop to this organization of more than 30,000 employees across the U.S. Our interactions with these employees at all levels provided us with valuable insights into the tremendous power of subtle behaviors.

We later designed and developed new workshops for other clients based on continuing research, and to reflect their unique industries, environments and corporate cultures. With thousands of interactions and discussions around this topic, we learned that participants wanted the microinequities conversation to be a very personal one.

They wanted their peers, supervisors, even family and friends to know what ticked them off. Because they wanted people to stop triggering them! Thus we coined the phrase MicroTrigger.

During these workshops, participants listed on flipcharts the MicroTriggers that most impacted them. Team leaders, managers, everyone wanted to take the flipcharts after the class. They wanted to hang them in their workspaces to remind the team which behaviors mattered most to their colleagues. They wanted the data. Clients asked how they as individuals, and how they as a group, compared to others who had also taken our workshops. They wanted more data.

So we launched the MicroTrigger Quiz. We developed four scenarios that had frequently been described in our classes. We asked, "Does this impact you? Does it matter who sends the MicroTrigger? Whether they are your boss or your peer? Whether they are older or younger? Your own gender or opposite?" Their responses provided more insights and much more data! People took the quiz and also took the time to write in comments about their other MicroTriggers. Four scenarios were not enough to describe the behaviors that impacted people. Knowing why people were triggered was as interesting as knowing what triggered them. We continued to conduct workshops, to listen to clients, to read comments and to ask, "What's Your MicroTrigger?" This book was born to share what we learned.

Even as we utilized the pre-publication version of the book, clients started ripping out pages. They wanted to tape their specific MicroTrigger on their cubicle wall, their office door, and even their forehead.

So each MicroTrigger page is now perforated (for easier ripping) and the book comes with a handy stand.

May you proudly display your MicroTrigger!

You'll feel better for sharing. And even better when others who care about you demonstrate it by treating you well as defined by you.

Janet Crenshaw Smith
October 2006

Both And

Micro things should be considered in a context of 'both and." Both the small things and the big things are important. Neither can be ignored. For example, when companies wish to recruit a more diverse workforce, where they recruit is a key factor in whether they will be successful. When recruiting on college campuses, having a presence at high caliber schools such as Morehouse and Spelman Colleges in Atlanta, for example, is as important as recruiting at schools such as Harvard or Yale. While where the company recruits is key, it is not enough. Equally important to successfully recruiting diverse talent are "little things." Consider the following scenario:

You are a part of a team of interviewers and are having a very successful interview with a graduate of Howard University. The interview is going well and the candidate, Jonathan, has really been able to sell himself. You are sure that your company is his first choice and know that your boss is equally impressed. Just then, your boss says, "Jonathan, you'd really fit in here. You bring diversity and you are so articulate." Jonathan ignores the comment but looks deflated and thanks you for your time. After the interview, your boss says that although Jonathan has excellent qualifications, his attitude might not be an asset.

In this scenario the comment, "You're so articulate" was a negative MicroTrigger for the candidate. For some, such a comment is a little thing. Yet in this case, it was important enough to a candidate that it soured the interview—for both the candidate and the prospective employer. We've observed that MicroTrigger #42, "You're so articulate" or "You speak so well", is frequently received as a message of lowered expectations. People of color, people born outside the U.S., and people who hold lower level jobs have said to us, "How many times have you heard someone say that a White man is articulate?"

While it would be easier to focus only on big or little, overt or subtle, **Both and** is significantly more effective.

Baring My Soul

When I tell you my
MicroTrigger,
I reveal myself to you. That
is a gift. In essence, I tell
you what makes me tick.
How I define respect, what's
important to me, who is
important to me.

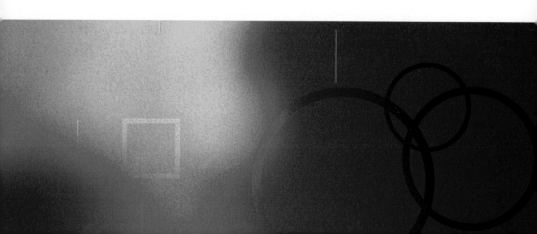

A clerical worker shared that she was not triggered when the company supervisors failed to say, "Hello" to her. Yet she was very impacted when her peer-level co-workers exhibited the same behavior. Why? "I don't expect much of the executives here. But my peers? They are important to me." WOW.

Understanding the who, what and why of MicroTriggers requires good giving and good receiving. This open communication may not come easy. The triggers that have bounced amongst a team may have damaged trust in that group. The motivation to give the gift of "baring one's soul" comes from the hope of improving work relationships, improving the workplace. The good news is that many people are willing to take the plunge. Even if they have tolerated what they feel is unpleasant or unfair treatment. They will "risk" having the MicroTrigger conversation in order to reap future rewards like:

> Being treated with more respect as they define it

> Feeling included in ways that are meaningful to them

> Knowing that they are contributing to a more inclusive workplace

Demonstrating Leadership

Companies use similar words to describe the leadership competencies and behaviors they believe will create a productive and desirable place to work. Behaviors such as:

> Respect

> Teamwork

> Leadership

> Inclusion

Yet people sometimes struggle with how to measure leadership competencies. People say, "I know when it's there, and I know when it isn't." As the makeup of the workforce continues to change, it is increasingly important to learn how to self-manage subtle behaviors and to manage those dynamics in a team environment.

My manager does not respect me. She INTERRUPTS ME.

Our team is dysfunctional. My colleague ONLY REPLIES TO MY EMAILS WHEN A MANAGER IS COPIED ON IT.

Whether you manage hundreds of employees or you are a member of a team, you demonstrate leadership when you show that you understand the impact of subtle behaviors.

Why Does That Trigger You?

A great deal of power lies behind the implied meaning of MicroTriggers. It's not just the behavior. It's what it means to you when someone exhibits that behavior. For example,

FREQUENTLY CONFUSING YOU WITH THE ONLY OTHER PERSON OF A SIMILAR DEMOGRAPHIC for some is not simply mistaken identity.

"People are so proud to say, 'I don't see color. I treat everyone the same.' So how the heck are they going to confuse me with Sue, the only other Asian woman in our whole department? We don't even look alike! That says to me, 'that's all I see when I see you. You're just one of those Asian women that we hired. I don't see you as an individual person.' That is disrespectful."

Understanding "why" a little thing has a big impact can be enlightening.

According to Fortune 500 Executive Coach, Judith E. Glaser, human beings share a set of Universal Fears and Desires (see box). Consider the "fear of being excluded (rejected)." Glaser notes that this fear often prompts people to "create 'old boy networks' and exclude others first." NEVER INVITING YOU TO JOIN THE GROUP FOR LUNCH, MicroTrigger #33 may trigger you because of your human desire to be included on a winning team. It's not the action itself that is troublesome. Many people enjoy eating lunch alone at their desks. It is the underlying feeling – often a fear or a desire – that has the BIG impact.

Universal Fears and Desires

Universal Fears	Universal Desires
Being excluded (rejected) . . . so we create "old-boy networks" and exclude others first.	Being included on a winning team.
Being judged unfairly . . . so we criticize and blame others.	Being appreciated and acknowledged.
Failing . . . so we avoid taking risks and making mistakes.	Being successful.
Losing power . . . so we intimidate others to get power.	Being powerful.
Feeling stupid . . . so we either don't speak up or speak too much; or make others stupid.	Being smart, creative and a contributor.
Looking bad (embarrassed) in front of others . . . so we save face.	Being a leader with a valued voice.
Having no passion or meaning.	Being important and part of something bigger than you alone.

From Creating We, Change I-Thinking to WE-Thinking and Build a Healthy, Thriving Organizaiton by Judith E. Glaser

Is there a playbook?

I am sometimes asked for a list of the top five or ten MicroTriggers. People want a playbook: Avoid these words, these behaviors, and you're done. It is not that simple. I do recommend that you learn and post Your Team's MicroTriggers. But you must be careful to include the MicroTriggers that don't make the top ten list, yet are important to an individual in your group.

MicroTriggers are personal.

Asking someone, "How was your weekend?" may be a positive trigger for you. Yet it may be a negative one for someone else.

I may be triggered when some groups exclude me. Yet not when others do.

If you take this topic seriously, then you should be willing to take the time to understand the nuances. The "easy categories, check off a list" approach won't work for this. It requires a commitment to take the time to learn about yourself and your colleagues. Well worth the time.

Why Are Most Of The MicroTriggers NEGATIVE?

We tried to balance negative MicroTriggers with positive ones. We even took the positive voice on some that were at first negative. (#33 "how about lunch?" versus "never asks me to lunch") because deep down I'm a very optimistic and positive person. And people broke it down for us. Most people said that the negative triggers were more impactful for them than the positive ones. Yikes!

Roles And Responsibilities

MicroTriggers happen. When they do, what to do? Make yourself responsible for making a move, for taking an action, for doing something. What you do depends upon your role: are you the sender of the MicroTrigger, the receiver of the MicroTrigger, or an observer of what took place? Regardless of your role, you can take responsibility for Knowing Yourself, Taking Ownership, and Developing Your Roadmap.

Sender Responsibilities:

Watch your interactions:	Communicate:
Are they different or the same for others in similar situations?	Have you communicated and acknowledged sending micro-inequities?
Have you discounted or invalidated the contributions made?	Have you discussed your intent versus the impact of your action, without diminishing the importance of the impact?
Do you multi-task with some and not others?	Have you created an environment where others feel empowered to speak up and identify microinequities?
Do you seem to have time for some and not others?	Have you asked if you are creating and sustaining an inclusive work environment?
Does your body language accurately convey your message?	Are you able to admit to others that you are unsure how to effectively communicate with them?
Do you consistently use a tone and language that is respectful?	Can others trust you not to be angry, hurt, and/or retaliate if they are honest with you?

Receiver Responsibilities:

Know Yourself	Take Ownership
Watch your interactions:	**Respond in ways that encourage positive interactions:**
Have you assessed whether or not the behavior is one of your MicroTriggers?	Have you communicated the impact the behavior has on you and your performance?
Are you triggered by some Senders and not by others?	Are you able to respond in a respectful manner?
Have you frequently been a recipient of micro-inequities? Or is this a new experience for you?	Have you asked for clarification and/or a better understanding of the intent behind the message you received?

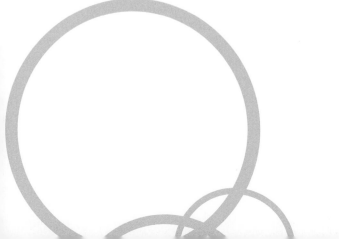

Observer Responsibilities:

Know Yourself	Take Ownership
Watch your interactions:	**Consider actions that provide an objective perspective and preserve relationships:**
Have you assessed whether or not the behavior is one of your own MicroTriggers?	Is this an environment in which it is safe to speak up?
Are you sometimes silent when you observe microinequities in order to protect or improve your own position?	Have you considered discussing the situation "offline" with the sender?
Do you sometimes ignore micro-inequities sent by others, because they are same ones that you send?	Have you asked the Receiver if and/or how they would have wanted you to respond?

Create an Environment for the Conversation

How liberating it can be to tell someone, "That's my MicroTrigger!" Like taking a tiny pebble out of our shoe, it's getting rid of a little thing that's been very annoying. A manager said, "I have incorrectly been calling Lisa by the name Tina for the last nine months. Finally someone corrected me." Imagine how Lisa had been feeling. And why did it take nine months for someone to correct the manager?! FEAR. Your colleagues will not tell you that you have triggered them if they fear that you will not receive it well. Their fears include fear of conflict, retaliation, hurting feelings, thinking you're a whiner... To make this work, you must create an environment for the conversation.

Give the group permission to have the conversation. Acknowledge that the conversation can be challenging, but that the rewards are worth it. Create a signaling system. When you introduce language, such as "That's a MicroTrigger!" "That's my MicroTrigger!" that the group starts to adopt, it makes it easier to signal that something happened.. The conversation starts to become a normal part of your group's culture.

MicroTrigger>

1

Not speaking to you

Your co-worker comes in every morning and spends time greeting and talking with other co-workers on the floor but never says anything to you – not even a hello.

MicroTrigger>

2

Interrupting you

You notice that when you are speaking, whether in a meeting or during general conversation, your co-worker cuts you off mid-sentence and does not let you finish your thoughts.

MicroTrigger>

3

Leaving your name off the e-mail distribution list

MicroTrigger>

4

Questioning your qualifications

You contribute your comments and suggestions. The response? "Great idea. Did you think of that yourself?"

MicroTrigger> 5

Not introducing you

MicroTrigger> 6

Frequently asking you questions about your demographic as if you are the expert

MicroTrigger>

7

Never remembering your name

or (having met you several times before) never remembering that they have met you

MicroTrigger> 8

Responding to your question with,

"Didn't you read your email?"

rather than simply answering your question.

MicroTrigger> 9

Taking phone calls during a meeting with you

MicroTrigger>

10

Never asking,

"How was your weekend?," inquiring about your family or showing that they care about your personal interests

MicroTrigger>

11

Singling you out to ask for your.....

- Employee I. D.
- Driver's License
- Boarding Pass

At work. The rules say that everyone should always wear his or her employee identification in clear view. But most people don't. Your co-workers stroll past the security desk into the building. But the security guard singles you out saying, "I.D. please."

At the store. You present your credit card to purchase an item. The clerk asks you (but hasn't asked the others before you) for your driver's license when you make a credit card purchase.

At the airport. By the time you board the airplane, you've shown your boarding pass at least 3 times. Yet the flight attendant asks you, only you, for your boarding pass.

MicroTrigger> 12

Referring to women as "girls" or "gals"

MicroTrigger>

13

Restating your words for you

"What she means is..." Did anyone ask you to explain what I meant? Who named you the official translator? If someone wants to know what I meant, let them ask me. I can speak for myself thank you very much.

MicroTrigger>

14

Always sitting behind their desk when having conversations with you

but moving to the side table or couch for conversations with them

MicroTrigger> 15

Asking someone else the same question that you just answered for them

MicroTrigger>

16

Speaking more slowly or loudly to you than to others

MicroTrigger>

17

Saying,

"You don't talk or look

"

———————————————

(fill in the blank with your
dimension of diversity)

MicroTrigger>

18

Sighing when you ask a question

MicroTrigger>

19

Rolling their eyes at you

MicroTrigger>

20

Having insider jokes....
and not letting you in

Everyone's laughing. Something is funny.

But you don't let me in on the joke?

What is that about????

MicroTrigger>

21

Referring to younger adults as "kids"

MicroTrigger>

22

Remarks such as,

"That's administrative work"

MicroTrigger>

23

Only replying to your emails when a manager is copied on it too

MicroTrigger>

24

Greeting others in a traditional manner such as "Hi. Nice to meet you." and despite not knowing you,

Greeting you in an ethnically familiar manner

such as "Hey, Wazup!" (to Black coworkers) or "¿Que Pasa?" (to Latino coworkers).

MicroTrigger>

25

Always holding meetings at their location (floor, office, site, etc.)

58 little things that have a BIG impact

MicroTrigger>

26

Acknowledging your idea only after someone else restates it

© 2006 Ivy Planning Group

MicroTrigger>

27

Calling you by a nickname that they created for you

When a name is unfamiliar to someone or difficult for someone to pronounce, rather than take the time to learn how to pronounce it, some people take a route that is simpler for them. They change the name!

They shorten the name so that they can pronounce it.

Or decide to call you by your initials. So Filipe becomes "Phil", Jorge becomes "J", ...

Other times, people just decide that they like the nickname better than your given name. So James becomes "Jim", Michael becomes "Micky", Candessa becomes "Candi".....

MicroTrigger>

28

Not believing that you can perform a difficult task

MicroTrigger>

29

Referring to a group as, "You People"

MicroTrigger>

30

Arriving late to meetings or keeping you waiting

MicroTrigger>

31

Assuming that you are a secretary

YES. I KNOW. The fact that this is someone's MicroTrigger could indeed be YOUR MicroTrigger! Am I saying that being a secretary is a bad thing? Absolutely NOT. It is a valuable job AND sometimes people are triggered when others assume that they are the secretary.

Other examples we've heard are: support positions, non-management roles, cleaning staff, etc.

MicroTrigger>

32

Frequently confusing you with someone else of the same demographic

MicroTrigger>

33

Never inviting you to join the group for lunch

I'll never forget the following email I received from a class participant.

"Thank you so much your Inclusion Workshop last week. For the first time since I came to this new department, my co-workers asked me if I'd like to join them for lunch. I couldn't believe how good it made me feel!"

MicroTrigger>

34

Saying,

"I can't tell that joke. We're in mixed company."

MicroTrigger>

35

Asking others about their experiences or opinions but never asking you

MicroTrigger>

36

Scheduling meetings at times that they know you are not available

MicroTrigger> 37

Typing on the computer, blackberry, palm, etc... when talking to you

MicroTrigger>

38

Looking at their watch repeatedly during a conversation with you

MicroTrigger>

39

Calling you

"dear" "sweetheart" "honey" or "love"

MicroTrigger>

40

Using acronyms, jargon, or examples that exclude you

MicroTrigger>

41

Saying, "You look nice today."

MicroTrigger>

42

Remarks such as ...

"You're so articulate." or
"You speak so well."

MicroTrigger>

43

When disagreeing with you,

Stating their opinion as a fact using phrases such as

"Everyone knows that..." or "Well, obviously..."

MicroTrigger>

44

Not inviting you to represent the organization at a company-sponsored event

MicroTrigger>

45

Frequently asking you, "Are you sure?"

MicroTrigger>

46

Having a side conversation in a meeting when you are speaking

MicroTrigger>

47

Not looking you in the eye when speaking to you

MicroTrigger>

48

Looking past you when they're talking to you

We're at a gathering, having a conversation. Rather than focus on our conversation, you're constantly looking past me. The message: "if someone better comes along, I'm outta here."

If you want to be with me, be with me. If you don't, don't be so obvious.

58 little things that have a BIG impact

MicroTrigger>

49

Patting you on the back

MicroTrigger>

50

Discussing a social event that included everyone except you

MicroTrigger>

51

Getting physically close to you and/or touching you when speaking

MicroTrigger>

52

Shaking your hand too softly, or....much too hard

MicroTrigger> 53

Not inviting you to the impromptu meeting

Sometimes important decisions are made in unplanned meetings. When time is of the essence – which is often the case in today's fast-paced world – people gather with very little notice. How nice when YOU are the one who is tapped to join the "ad hoc" "impromptu" "it just kinda happened" meeting.

MicroTrigger>

54

Using too many sports analogies

MicroTrigger>

55

Referring to men as "boys"

MicroTrigger> 56

Not saying "Thank You"

MicroTrigger>

57

Taking credit for your work

Yesterday, you overheard your co-worker tell someone else about a fantastic idea they had. Only problem, the idea was yours. You had recommended it to your co-worker a few days before.